GO!

10 POWERFUL STEPS TO ACCOMPLISHING
YOUR GOALS &
LIVING THE LIFE YOU DESIRE

GO!

10 POWERFUL STEPS TO ACCOMPLISHING YOUR GOALS & LIVING THE LIFE YOU DESIRE

Dr. Cherita Weatherspoon

Weatherspoon Publishing
BEAR, DELAWARE

GO! 10 Powerful Steps to Accomplishing Your Goals & Living the Life You Desire
Copyright © 2016 by Cherita G. Weatherspoon
ISBN 978-0-9983130-2-3 (ebook)
ISBN 978-0-9983130-0-9 (paperback)
Library of Congress Control Number: 2016919807

All rights reserved. No part of this publication may be reproduced, distributed, stored in a retrieval system, or transmitted in any form or by any means, including photocopying, recording, or other electronic or mechanical methods, without the prior written permission of the publisher, except for brief quotations in critical reviews, articles, or certain noncommercial uses permitted by copyright law. For permission requests, write to the publisher, at:
Weatherspoon Publishing
Attention: Permissions Request
P.O. Box 11282
Wilmington, DE 19850

Legal Disclaimer
This book is for informational purposes only. The author makes no claims or guarantees of outcomes or success. The content in this book should not be considered as counseling or other professional advice. Readers may implement the information included at their own discretion.

Cover Photo: Michael Nicholls Photography

Ordering Information
Go! may be purchased in large quantities at a discount for educational, business or sales promotional use. For information, email info@cheritaweatherspoon.com.

Request Cherita
To request Dr. Cherita Weatherspoon for a keynote address, speaking engagement, workshop, seminar, orientation, or as your personal or executive coach or consultant, visit www.cheritaweatherspoon.com or email info@cheritaweatherspoon.com.

*To those who have been delayed, denied and dismissed;
but never stopped dreaming.*

Rave Reviews

'After reading GO, I found myself engaged in a life changing self-evaluation that would spark a desire to move further towards my purpose. GO offers tangible ways to be free from standing still. Dr. Weatherspoon provides attention-grabbing instruction that is direct yet gentle in its approach. Fasten your seatbelt, because GO will definitely take you on a life-changing ride!"

-Dr. Malaika Turner, Founder, Motivation That Moves

"Cherita Weatherspoon's GO provides us with an inspirational, practical, fail-proof guide for how to initiate the process of real change in our lives. Honest, deep, self-reflection is without question one of the disciplines that absolutely all successful people consistently employ in their lives and in their work. In ten quick, fun, immediately effective steps, GO gets you refocused, reflecting, motivated and prepared to accomplish your goals and to change your life. You are smart to both read and share this book with your families, friends and the teams you lead because the strategies in it enable you to inject positive change into your business and into your life right away!"

-Je'neen Barlow, Author, Speaker, Executive Coach, Barlow Enterprises

"Dr. Weatherspoon offers ten practical steps to help the reader reach his/her goals. I found GO to be thought-provoking and inspirational. She challenges the reader to dig deep within to answer tough questions, thereby enabling the reader to push past obstacles. GO is a simple, yet powerful guide to fulfilling your purpose. I can already see myself recommending this roadmap to friends and colleagues."

-Lisa Lewis, Vice President Seeds of Greatness
Ministries; Founder *Girlfriends!*

"In GO, you have a 'one stop shop' for motivation, reflection and engagement. This is an inspiring and dynamic manuscript which should be required reading for anyone looking to propel their life, career or ministry to the next level. Engaging and well written are the best ways to describe this book, in my opinion. I highly recommend!"

-Dr. Melvin Jenkins, Founder & Bishop
Victory Christian Assembly; Professor & Chairperson,
IUP Dept. of Developmental Studies

'GO serves as a beautiful conduit for anyone who finds themselves stuck and stagnate between who they are now and who they ultimately want to become. As an entertainment correspondent, producer and content creator whose job is to deliver high profile in depth celebrity interviews across global multiple media platforms along with negotiating contracts with media elites in Hollywood, New York, and London, I have found the coaching offered in this workbook by Dr. Weatherspoon bar none. In order to execute at the highest level of my craft and sustain in the ever changing but always competitive space of entertainment news, it is imperative that I continue to implement the 10 components of Dr. Weatherspoon's GO strategy. In a point by point layout that consists of awareness and accountability for one's own actions, Dr. Weatherspoon has successfully laid out a blueprint of characteristics that prepares the reader to want success, embrace success, and expect success. Her instructions require work and patience. But, more importantly, her instructions will guide you to the epicenter of opportunity and the ability to be like hinds and place your feet on high places."

-Tanisha LaVerne Grant,
Independent Entertainment Correspondent

"From the start, I was drawn into critical reflection. Having spent years sifting through different tools for self-care, for help to live the life I want and am living on purpose and to be self-less in my care of the world around me, I found the very first step familiar, and necessary, and still drawn to think deeply about whether I have indeed grown as much as possible in regard to rising above past hurt and pain. GO asks you to consider questions that may be unparalleled in any other coaching tool. 'Is whatever is holding you back WORTH giving away your power or sacrificing your dreams?' There are success super powers and GO acknowledges that they are in you and helps you unleash them as if you are in life coaching sessions. This tool puts life coaching at the fingertips of millions and better yet, you can work through this 10 step process over and over and over again for any personal, professional or business goals. Get ready, get set, GO!"

-Rochelle Peterson-Ansari, Educational Leadership Specialist, Trainer, Perceptions Unlimited

'Grab this book and guarantee the success you deserve. It is pining to generate wider and more succinct options needed to practically birth sustainable goals--yours! Dr. Weatherspoon has gifted the world with an unparalleled resource certain to weed out procrastination, underdog delay and bring balance to your success ladder. She masterfully devised thought provoking nuggets immediately followed by introspective "growth mindset" questions which jolt, challenge and catapult all willing to delve beyond today's sight lines. This G-10 force' will powerfully stand-up in you. The proof easily speaks through Dr. Weatherspoon's living witness, extends to her family success and thrives among all who adhere to Dr. Weatherspoon's counsel and coaching; gleaning in pursuit of purpose fulfilled! It's your time, now GO forth!'

-LaTerra D. Ruffin MDiv, CPE, CPMLC, Lead Pastor, Life Empowerment Church

"GO is an amazing and powerful guide that will inspire you to press forward to accomplish your goals and live the life you desire despite the challenges that may be in your way. Dr. Weatherspoon has provided us with ten practical steps to take your life to the next level. If you're ready for the change you've been craving, GO is a must read for you. Get ready to experience your breakthrough."

-Joyce Dungee Proctor, Speaker, Leading Career Development Strategist, Coach and Author, Seminars By Joyce – The Total You, Inc.

"Dr. Cherita Weatherspoon delivers a wonderfully prescriptive self-help strategy for goal attainment. Through this brilliantly and beautifully written manuscript, she provides the reader with a user-friendly method to GO forward and accomplish their vision and dreams. The book offers a variety of exercises, including self-assessments, which allow the reader to reprioritize goals and objectives when necessary, and strategically plan for better life outcomes."

'In many ways, the manuscript is motivational and transformative. Dr. Weatherspoon gives the reader the courage to part with current vices and rediscover opportunity, vigor and excitement. This book is not a one read manuscript. GO has an amazing residual effect for the consumer. It is a high value resource and an infinite repository of wisdom and guidance. In addition, the manuscript is a wonderful road map for all readers to rediscover their dreams and secure their future through Dr. Weatherspoon's groundbreaking GO strategy and methodology. This is a 'must read' for all who have aspirations that have not yet come to pass. The text is accessible for all readers. Dr. Weatherspoon has offered a transformative game-changer from the word GO!"

-Dr. Anthony Driggers, Founder
Options Without Walls, LLC

I have learned that if one advances in the direction of his dreams, and endeavors to live the life he has imagined, he will meet with a success unexpected in common hours.

— Henry David Thoreau

Contents

Foreword

Acknowledgements

Introduction

Step 1: Get Over 1

Step 2: Get On 9

Step 3: Get Obsessed 19

Step 4: Give Out 29

Step 5: Grab Opportunities 39

Step 6: Go On 49

Step 7: Gamble Occasionally 59

Step 8: Gaze Over 69

Step 9: Goof Off 77

Step 10: Game On 87

Foreword

When you think about goals and the real steps to accomplishing them, I believe we can all talk about all the ways we've tried in the past. After all, if you felt like you had a handle on achieving your goals you probably would have never considered picking up this book; however, because you did, it tells me a couple of things. First, you have goals that you would like to accomplish and just haven't met them yet; and second, you have done it all before -had a goal, started on a path to achieve it, followed the goal plan and then… crickets; another year has passed and you still have that same "dream deferred".

As a teacher of goal setting and manifesting dreams, I thought I had explored every aspect of how to accomplish them. In *GO*, Dr. Weatherspoon has developed a new strategy for creating lasting change in your life by taking it to the next level. These 10 steps are not goal setting as usual. It forces you to **_Reflect_**, which allows you to explore your thoughts and feelings, **_Identify_** what you have done or what you plan to do, **_Clarify_** by exploring a new perspective, and **_Act_** by creating a practical action plan to implement your new found knowledge.

The writing exercises after each brief lesson allows one to explore the things you really need to consider. Science concludes that writing about your goals helps make sense of what you are working toward and what may have prevented success in the past. The physical act of writing down a goal makes it real and tangible. You have no excuse for forgetting about it. This book, though, is more than just SMART goals. The **Act** step is often missed in the process of goal setting. You get so focused on the outcome that you forget to plan all of the steps that are needed along the way. By writing it out as you read, you will literally be crossing each one off as you complete it, you'll realize that you are making progress towards your ultimate goal. This is especially important if your goal is big and demanding. *GO* will set you up for long-term and life changing success.

If you're tired of trying to achieve your goals in the same way you've been taught and coming up empty, then this book is for you. It is a new approach that, if followed, can significantly change your life.

Goal setting is much more than simply saying you want something to happen. If you clearly define exactly what you want, understand why you want it in the first place, and with this book explore the deeper things that may be holding you back through journaling, the likelihood of your success is greatly increased.

Dr. Cherita Weatherspoon leads by example and *GO*

comes from her very own recipe book of success. By following *GO*, you can set goals with confidence and enjoy the satisfaction that comes along with knowing you achieved what you set out to do.

Allison T. Butler, The Prison Break Coach

Acknowledgements

To the God who gives every good and perfect gift, I praise and worship you. To my husband, Gary, who allows me to dream and to do, I love you. To my children, Emile, Corban, Jaden and Ian, thank you for giving me the time -your time -to do what I've been called to do. Thank you to my friend, Lois Miller, who offers excellent support and feedback. And, to the women who have motivated me simply by being who they are and stepping out in faith and on purpose, Dr. Malaika Turner, Otishia Emmens, Michelle Washington, Allison Butler, Je'neen Barlow, Raphaela Browne, Nisa Williams, Jil Jordan Greene, Rev. LaTerra Ruffin, Tanisha LaVerne Grant and Angelita Byrd, you never know who's watching or how much of an impact you are making. Thank you for forging the path.

Introduction

It is one thing to talk about and envision your future and to know where you want to go, but it is a totally different thing to know how to get from where you are to where you want to be. It is one thing to develop SMART goals and know the steps to take to accomplish your goals, but a totally different thing to know how to deal with the challenges that you will face as you work towards meeting your goals.

You see, no matter how well you can write out or state a SMART goal, it is not enough to move you from where you are to where you want to be. Having a plan is not enough. Having an accountability partner, a mentor or friend who can help keep you on track, is not enough.

I am not telling you not to set goals, not to make sure they are SMART goals, not to write them down, not to plan or not to find people to help you along the way. What I am telling you, however, is that there are going to be challenges that come your way and threaten to thwart your progress, get you off track, and in some cases totally destroy you. Some of these challenges will come simply because of the goals you have set, some will come because of decisions and choices you make that are not in your own best interest, others will come because some of the people in your life will not want to see you "make it," and still others will come simply because challenges, issues and problems are a part of life and everyone has something to deal with. No matter how good a person's life may seem from the outside looking in, I can guarantee you that everyone has had some stuff to deal with as they have worked towards reaching their goals.

So, if everyone has some stuff to deal with, why is it that some people accomplish what they set out to accomplish and others do not? Why are some people successful while others fail? I believe it is because some people understand what the Go, G - O, in goal really means. *GO! 10 Powerful Steps To Accomplishing Your Goals & Living The Life You Desire* is designed to help you deal with the stuff that keeps you from setting or accomplishing your goals. Through this life application journal, you will identify the things (and people) that have been distracting and deterring you. You will learn to release emotional baggage, relax and enjoy YOU, and you will develop the skills and the fortitude to make it into that small percentage of people who actually set and accomplish their goals.

But, remember, for real change to occur, you will have to take action. You will need to do something –you will need to *GO!* This life application journal will help you do just that. My recommendation is to read through each step before going back to complete the journal entries. This will give you a clear understanding of the process and allow you to see how the steps work collaboratively to move you forward. Keep in mind that while this is a process and there are steps involved, the steps do not necessarily occur in sequential order. You may not work totally through one step before beginning the next; and some steps, like Gaze Over and Goof Off, are steps that you should repeat throughout the process. Adapt these steps as a continuous and perpetual approach to achieving your goals.

In each step a description of what is necessary to move forward is provided. You are then asked to **Reflect** on what you've read –sharing both your thoughts and your feelings. Then you'll move to very powerful and pointed questions that will help you to **Identify** the things that have been influencing you, holding you back, distracting you, or otherwise inhibiting your progress. The next section asks questions that will help you to **Clarify** where you are now and how you want or need to move forward. Finally, each step asks you to **Act**.

It is your commitment to taking the time to respond to these questions and then to implement them in your life that will make the difference in where you are today and where you will be 12 months from now. It is a small thing that brings about a major impact. It won't take a lot of time, but it will take a lot of heart. This is soul work. Are you ready? I'm with you, let's GO!

Cherita

I've always found that anything worth achieving will always have obstacles in the way and you've got to have the drive and determination to overcome those obstacles on route to whatever it is that you want to accomplish.

— Chuck Norris

STEP 1

Get Over

*Getting over a painful experience is much like crossing monkey bars.
You have to let go at some point
in order to move forward.
- C.S. Lewis*

Are you living a fairy tale life? Do you have everything you could dream of and would not change one thing about your life? Or, have you have been disappointed or hurt by people you love and care about? Do you feel like life has not been fair to you? If so, this first step is for you.

Get Over.

Whether it was a friend, boyfriend, parent, sibling, spouse, boss or co-worker -whoever it was that hurt you, Get Over it. Whatever you didn't like, whatever made you mad, or whatever the situation that was not fair or right. Get Over it. No, you did not deserve it. No, they did not apologize. Yes, you are angry and it still hurts; but hanging on to whatever it is, is only hurting you. Focusing on past, and even present, pain will keep you from your future goals. Whatever that thing is that has you constantly talking and thinking about yesterday, last month, last year, or five years ago - Get Over it.

Getting over it doesn't mean you forget about what happened, but it does mean that you rise above it. How do you that? Let's get to work.

React

What is your immediate reaction to what you've just read? What thoughts came to mind? What feelings did you experience?

_____
_____
_____
_____
_____
_____
_____
_____
_____
_____

Identify

Who are the people that hurt you that you have not forgiven?

_____
_____
_____
_____
_____
_____
_____
_____
_____
_____
_____

Why is it difficult for you to forgive them?

_____
_____
_____
_____
_____
_____
_____
_____

Have they moved on from the problem/situation? How do you know?

_____
_____
_____
_____
_____
_____
_____
_____

Clarify
What benefit does not forgiving them bring you?

_____
_____

What are you missing out on because a part of your life - a part of your heart, is stuck in the past?

Is it worth it? What is it about this person or this situation that makes you willing to give away your power and/or your joy?

Act

Speak your PEACE. If the person is accessible and it is safe for you to do so, talk to them directly. Otherwise, it is just as powerful to verbalize this while looking in a mirror or at a photo of the person. Say the following, filling in the blanks based on your experience:

I feel hurt when _____
_____
_____
_____
_____.

*I felt*_____
_____
_____
_____;

and it has bothered me since it happened. But today, I am letting it go. I can no longer give your actions any power in my life. I can no longer allow this situation to continue to bring me pain. I forgive you, and I also forgive myself for not letting go of this anger and hurt sooner. I am worth so much more than this.

If this isn't enough for you, go to a private place, throw something, yell, cry, cuss; but whatever you do, make the decision (and it is a decision) to Get Over it. Clinging to the past, holding unforgiveness in your heart does not serve you in any positive way.

Don't talk about the person or the situation again. Don't let other people pull you into a conversation about it. When it creeps into your mind, speak aloud, "I am over it.

It is not worth my time or energy." Then, say this short affirmation:

I am free from anger and fear. I am guided by love and I forgive freely. Because love fills my heart, good things come my way.

One of the most courageous decisions you'll ever make is to finally let go of what is hurting your heart and soul.

- Brigitte Nicole

STEP 2

Get On

*There are far, far better things ahead than any
we leave behind.
- C.S. Lewis*

After you Get Over, it is now time to Get On. Get On with your life. Begin to live like you have a future beyond your current or past situation, because you do. It is not enough to get over something -to rise above it; while you may be operating at a higher level, you are still lingering in the same general area. Maybe you have stopped talking about whatever it was. You may have even forgiven the wrong that was done to you; but you are not ready to try again, to trust again, to love again.

After you Get Over, you have to Get On with it. You have to be about making the life that YOU want to live, not the life that just happens to be thrown at you. Get On with going back to college. Get On with getting that job at the company you have always wanted to work for. Get On with relocating to Florida or the ATL, or Cali, or wherever it is you have always dreamt of living. Get On with starting that business you have been planning on paper for all these years. Get On with turning your side hustle into a legitimate business. Get On with introducing yourself to that man or woman you see every day at lunch, church or wherever, that always smiles at you; but you are too afraid to respond because of the person you just realized you needed to Get Over. Get On with it. Get On with living your life.

React

What is your immediate reaction to what you've just read? What thoughts came to mind? What feelings did you experience?

_____
_____
_____
_____
_____
_____
_____
_____
_____
_____

Identify

Where do you feel stuck in life, like you just can't get past this point?

_____
_____
_____
_____
_____
_____
_____
_____
_____
_____
_____

What do you think is holding you back?
_____
_____
_____
_____
_____
_____
_____
_____
_____
_____

What is it that you want to do that you have not pursued?
_____
_____
_____
_____
_____
_____
_____
_____
_____
_____

What prevents you from pursuing those things?
_____
_____
_____
_____
_____
_____

If you could wave a wand, how would your life be different?

Clarify
Look at your previous answers. Are the reasons you stated about being stuck and not pursuing what you want within your control or out of your control? How?

If you believe the reasons are out of your control, think deeply about it and identify one thing in each area (where you are stuck in life and what you want to pursue) that you can do to impact the situation in a positive way.

_____
_____
_____
_____
_____
_____
_____
_____
_____
_____

How will your life be different if you take these actions?

_____
_____
_____
_____
_____
_____
_____
_____
_____
_____

What do you see in your future if you don't take these actions?

_____
_____

_____
_____
_____
_____
_____

Why are you worth taking action?

_____
_____
_____
_____
_____
_____
_____
_____
_____

Act

Write a deadline for completing each of the two actions you listed under *Identify* above. The deadline must be within 7 days. If there is no possible way to complete the action within 7 days (example: start college classes, but you are reading this in October) break the larger task into several smaller tasks and complete at least one of them in the next 7 days, and continue working on completing these tasks in 7-day increments until the larger task is completed.

Deadline for action 1: _____

Deadline for action 2: _____

Once completed, describe how it feels to have taken action in these areas.

_____
_____
_____
_____
_____
_____
_____
_____

Keep moving forward. Continue to identify areas where you want to move forward in your life – Get On. It can be in your work, relationships, family life, business, or any area in which you feel unfulfilled. Write those things below. You don't need to take action on all of them right now; but write them down as a reminder and after you have accomplished one of your first goals, come back to this list.

_____
_____
_____
_____
_____

The first step towards getting somewhere is to decide that you are not going to stay where you are.

- J.P. Morgan

STEP 3

Get Obsessed

Take up one idea. Make that one idea your life - think of it, dream of it, live on that idea. Let the brain, muscles, nerves, every part of your body, be full of that idea, and just leave every other idea alone. This is the way to success.
- Swami Vivekananda

You have gotten over the past hurt that kept you from looking towards your future and you have made the decision to start living and pursuing the things that you desire, but you have to get serious about going after what you want. Make a commitment to this pursuit.

Get Obsessed.

Think about your goals. Spend time planning out the steps you need to take to get where you want to be. Spend time each day doing something that gets you closer to your goal. Treat your goal like it is your new man or woman, your favorite sport, show, or another pursuit you love and invest in. Spend your free time on *it*. Talk about *it* to others, think about *it*, talk to yourself about *it*, turn things down that keep you from spending valuable time on *it* and that do not contribute at all to your success. Get Obsessed with *it*. Make *it* the number one priority in your life (after God), and your family. If you are not working on your goal, be learning more about what you need to achieve *it*. Research *it*, feed *it*, and nurture *it*. Get Obsessed with *it*. You will know when you are obsessed with *it* when people around you complain that *it* is all you talk about or that you are spending all your time on *it*. If you are not hearing that, you are not obsessed. You might have a crush on *it*, but you are not obsessed with *it*.

React
What is your immediate reaction to what you've just read? What thoughts came to mind? What feelings did you experience?

_____
_____
_____
_____
_____
_____
_____
_____
_____

Identify
What is *it* for you? What is the big dream?

_____
_____
_____
_____
_____
_____
_____
_____
_____
_____
_____

How much time are you currently spending on *it* on a daily basis? How about weekly?

_____
_____
_____
_____
_____
_____
_____
_____
_____
_____
_____
_____

Who knows about *it*? Who have you shared *it* with? (No, you cannot share your dreams with everybody, but you need to share *it* with somebody; otherwise *it* is just a secret and there is no accountability for you.)

_____
_____
_____
_____
_____
_____
_____
_____
_____
_____
_____

Clarify
Why does *it* matter to you?

_____
_____
_____
_____
_____
_____
_____
_____
_____

What are you willing to do to make *it* a reality?

_____
_____
_____
_____
_____
_____
_____
_____
_____

How will *it* change you or impact the world?

_____
_____
_____
_____

Act

Find additional time to work on *it*. Schedule this time on your calendar like you do other appointments. Make *it* a priority. This should be reflected in your schedule. When will you work on it?

_____
_____
_____
_____
_____
_____
_____
_____
_____
_____

Find two people who you can trust with your dreams and ask them to be your accountability partners. One should focus on holding you accountable for sticking to your schedule (share your schedule with them –just the days and times that you should be working on *it*) and the other should be focused on your progression –what and how much you are accomplishing.

Who will hold you accountable for sticking to your schedule and how will they do that?

_____
_____
_____
_____
_____
_____
_____

Who will hold you accountable for making progress on *it* and how will they do that?

_____
_____
_____
_____
_____
_____
_____

Speak life. Say something positive about *it* every day. What is your affirmation?

_____
_____

_____

_____

_____

_____

_____

Bring life. Do something related to *it* every day. What are you committed to doing on a daily basis?

*Determination becomes obsession and
then it becomes all that matters.*

- Jeremy Irvineare

DR. CHERITA WEATHERSPOON

BONUS GIFT

Sign up for the Spoonfed Motivation Blog at
https://cheritaweatherspoon.com/blog-subscription

STEP 4

Give Out

Remember that the happiest people are not those getting more, but those giving more.
- H. Jackson Brown, Jr.

The first three steps were rightfully and appropriately selfish, but this step is about other people. While the achievement of your goals is pretty much up to you and you have to put in the work, the reality is that no one does it on their own and it is not likely that others will help you if you are not willing to help others. Be willing to Give Out.

Give Out of your heart. Give Out of your talents. Give Out of your pain. There is someone who can use your help. It may be directly related to your goals, or it may simply be your presence for someone who is lonely, your words for someone who needs encouragement, your skills or talent for someone who cannot do something quite as well as you can. It may be volunteering with an organization or mentoring someone younger, or simply showing kindness or compassion. Giving out can take on many forms and it can be something big or small. It can be something you do every day or something that is done on a certain occasion. But whatever it is, whatever you have to offer -and you do have something to offer -Give Out of yourself to others and you will find that others, perhaps not the same people you helped, but others will give out of themselves to you.

React

What is your immediate reaction to what you've just read? What thoughts came to mind? What feelings did you experience?

_____
_____
_____
_____
_____
_____
_____
_____
_____

Identify

List your skills and talents.

_____
_____
_____
_____
_____
_____
_____
_____
_____
_____

How can you use your skills, talents, time or money to help someone else?

_____
_____
_____
_____
_____
_____
_____
_____
_____
_____

What groups of people do you want to help?

_____
_____
_____
_____
_____
_____
_____
_____
_____
_____

What causes are important to you?

_____
_____
_____
_____
_____

What organizations can you connect with that will allow you to use your skills, talent, time and/or money to support the people or causes that matter most to you?

Clarify
How could sharing your skills, talent, time and/or money enrich someone or a cause that matters to you?

How can this experience benefit you? What do you gain by giving out to others in this way?

How will you know that you have made a difference?

Act
Write down three to five organizations, groups, individuals or entrepreneurs that you know could benefit from your skills, talents, time or money.

_____
_____
_____
_____
_____
_____
_____
_____
_____

Contact each of them and offer what you have to offer them (skills, talent, time or money). Do not ask how you can help or if they need help. Tell them that you are contacting them because you to want to help by _____

_____
_____
_____
_____
_____
_____
_____
_____

Be specific about what you are offering (for example: developing their marketing materials for free, volunteering at their upcoming event, being a mentor with their youth program, presenting a workshop on choosing the right college, donating $100 to cover the cost of registration for a teenager to attend a leadership conference). The goal is to do something that matters to you in a way that utilizes your unique value while also benefiting the entity or person receiving from you. Be diligent and do not give up. It may take some time to work through approval processes; but keep calling until you have solidified the plan to Give Out or you have been told no.

Describe how being of service -giving out, felt to you.

_____
_____
_____
_____
_____
_____
_____
_____
_____
_____
_____
_____
_____
_____
_____
_____
_____

Now, set another date to do it again, either with the same organization/person or a different one to whom you can be of service.

As we work to create light for others, we naturally light our own way.

- Mary Anne Radmacher

STEP 5

Grab Opportunities

Fear stifles our thinking and actions. It creates indecisiveness that results in stagnation. I have known talented people who procrastinate indefinitely rather than risk failure. Lost opportunities cause erosion of confidence, and the downward spiral begins.
- Charles Stanley

When you develop your goals, you should have a plan for accomplishing them. However, your plan should not be so rigid that you cannot see how people or experiences outside of your plan can help further your progress towards your goals. Your plan cannot be so inflexible that it does not permit you a little discomfort when faced with something that is unfamiliar. You have to be willing to Grab Opportunities.

When it makes you nervous and takes you out of your comfort zone, Grab Opportunities. When it takes you into unfamiliar territory, Grab Opportunities. They may come when you least expect them, in a different form than you thought, and from a place or person that you never would have expected. But, do not turn away from opportunities because they were not a part of your plan. Plans can change, plans do change, plans will change. Control that change as much as possible by being open to unexpected opportunities. Don't turn away opportunities because it is different or new. That is what makes opportunities what they are. Do not turn away from them, grab them.

Don't mistake opportunities for distractions or distractions for opportunities. Distractions typically show up in the form of something that interests you or something that you should do because it's the right thing to do, but they do not directly relate to your goals or help to push you closer to your goals. Distractions take your time, energy and effort away from the pursuit of your goals. Opportunities, on the other hand, directly relate to your goal, help to advance your progress, expand your network, or build your skill set and knowledge as it relates to your goals. Avoid distractions, Grab Opportunities.

React
What is your immediate reaction to what you've just read? What thoughts came to mind? What feelings did you experience?

_____
_____
_____
_____
_____
_____
_____
_____

Identify
What opportunities have you let pass you by because it did not fit in with your timeline or plan?

_____
_____
_____
_____
_____
_____
_____
_____
_____

What opportunities have you missed because you did not think you were ready?

_____
_____
_____
_____
_____
_____
_____
_____
_____

What opportunities did you turn away from because you were afraid?

_____
_____
_____
_____
_____
_____
_____
_____
_____

What opportunities are open to you now?

_____
_____
_____

_____
_____
_____

What are you doing now that is a distraction from your goals?

_____
_____
_____
_____
_____
_____
_____
_____

Clarify

Making the choice to not take advantage of opportunities is typically for one of two reasons: control or fear. Either you want to be in control of what happens, when it happens and how it happens or you are afraid that it will not work out. If you did not create or initiate the opportunity, "it's not the right time," or you "don't have the time." If you are afraid, you wonder, "Can I do it?" "Am I ready?" or "What if?" Yes, these could be legitimate reasons and questions, but often they simply are not. They are excuses. So, what is your excuse? What prevents you from being open to new opportunities?

___

What is it about things not going as you planned that bothers you?

___

Why are you afraid?

___

_____
_____
_____
_____
_____
_____

Act
When an opportunity comes your way, ask yourself the following questions:

1. Is this related to my goals?
2. Could this increase the knowledge or skills I need to accomplish my goals?
3. Could this help me meet people who will help push my vision forward?
4. Could this propel me forward in the journey towards my goals?
5. Have I been preparing for this opportunity?
6. Will anyone die if I do this?
7. Will I lose my job or damage a relationship with someone I love if I do this?

If the answers to questions one through five are yes and the answers to six and seven are no, grab the opportunity.

Identify two to three recent opportunities that you did not take advantage of. Go back to the people who offered you the opportunities and ask if they are still available. List them on the next page and write down the outcome.

DR. CHERITA WEATHERSPOON

We must be willing to let go of the life we've planned, so as to have the life that is waiting for us.

- Joseph Campbell

STEP 6

Go On

*People fear leaving their safe harbor of the known and venturing off
into the unknown. Human beings crave certainty
- even when it limits them.
- Robin S. Sharma*

Now, with this step we are back to focusing on you. As you make progress towards accomplishing your goals, you are going to find that some of the people you thought cared about you start to think differently about you. You might hear them say things like, "You're changing," "You think you're better than everybody," "Since she started (<u>fill in the blank</u>) she ain't got time for nobody." That one is my favorite; because the thing is, they are right. You ain't got time for nobody, but you do have time for anybody who is trying to be somebody.

You will change and that is a good thing. In fact, it is a great thing! And, these people do care about you, but they are not sure what your change, your progression, and your goals mean for them. They are afraid that you will leave them behind. But you must know this one thing, you are not leaving anyone behind. They are choosing to stay behind. But you, you must Go On. Go On, despite what they think. Go On, despite what they say. Go On, because they cannot live for you. Go On, because you cannot live for them. Everyone has a choice to make about their lives and you cannot be nor are you responsible for another person's choices. If they choose to advance with you, hold out your hand and walk side-by-side towards your goals. But, if they choose to stay behind, you must Go On without them.

React

What is your immediate reaction to what you've just read? What thoughts came to mind? What feelings did you experience?

_____
_____
_____
_____
_____
_____
_____
_____
_____
_____
_____

Identify

What or who causes you to hesitate about making changes in your life that will advance you to the next level?

_____
_____
_____
_____
_____
_____
_____
_____
_____

What is so good about where you are now that you are willing to consider giving up everything waiting for you in your future?

_____
_____
_____
_____
_____
_____
_____
_____
_____
_____

What will you miss out on if you decide to stay behind instead of going on?

_____
_____
_____
_____
_____
_____
_____
_____
_____
_____

Clarify

How does playing small, staying who you are and continuing to do what you have been doing serve you?

GO!

_____
_____
_____
_____
_____
_____
_____

How does it serve those you love? (Hint: It does not, even if they think it does. You can be a much bigger help to them if you become who you are destined to be.)

_____
_____
_____
_____
_____
_____
_____
_____

If you stay behind, how will you feel about the people who discouraged you five years from now when you are stuck in the same situation that you are in today?

_____
_____
_____
_____

_____
_____
_____
_____
_____
_____

Act

Talk. Talk with the people you love who you feel are discouraging you from pursuing your goals. Find out why they are doing it? Share how it is affecting you. Reassure them that they can come with you, but that you must Go On. Share how it will impact you if you do not go after what you want. Then, ask about their dreams and desires –what it is they want to do. Encourage them to take the first steps towards making their dreams a reality. Set a date to talk with them and write those dates below.

_____
_____
_____
_____
_____
_____
_____
_____

Describe how it felt to have these conversations. Describe how you feel now about working towards your goals.

_____
_____
_____
_____
_____
_____
_____
_____

Guard your heart. If after talking with them, they continue to discourage you or they are generally unsupportive, limit what you share about what you are doing. Do not give them opportunity to discourage you or to sabotage you. Only share your goals and progress with those who will nurture it and help protect it. What if it is your spouse or significant other? If this is the case, you want to encourage healthy communication. Try developing a reasonable agreement around whatever their concerns are and establish boundaries that are respectful to both of you. Write below what you were able to come up with.

_____
_____
_____
_____
_____
_____

DR. CHERITA WEATHERSPOON

GO!

*You get a strange feeling
when you're about to leave a place,
like you'll not only miss the people
you love but you'll miss the person
you are now at this time
and this place, because
you'll never be this way again.*

- Azar Nafisi

DR. CHERITA WEATHERSPOON

BONUS GIFT

Get your complimentary *GO! 10 Step Process Infographic* to print and hang on your wall at https://cheritaweatherspoon.com/infographic

STEP 7

Gamble Occasionally

*If you are not willing to risk the unusual,
you will have to settle for the ordinary.
- Jim Rohn*

When you are working towards a goal, you will have to make decisions along the way. Some of these decisions will be very clear cut and it will be easy to know what you should do. Other decisions will not be as clear or may involve some risk. Be willing to Gamble Occasionally. Now, I don't mean to risk everything you have for a "sure thing," but I do mean that you need to be willing to take some risks to advance your cause. You will not always know what the outcome of a decision or choice will be. You will be called on to risk time, to risk effort, to risk money and every now and then you will need to take that risk -to Gamble Occasionally.

"What if" is a wicked game. What if I do this? But, what if I do that? What if this happens? But, what if it does not? None of us knows for sure what the future holds, but we do know that not taking any action means that you will not progress. Too many people choose not to act out of fear of loss or failure. Risk is not a bad thing. You just need to be smart about the risks you take. Do your homework, ask questions, weight out probable scenarios and then make an educated and informed decision. Don't take unnecessary or crazy risks, but be willing to Gamble Occasionally when the reward outweighs the risks.

React
What is your immediate reaction to what you've just read? What thoughts came to mind? What feelings did you experience?

_____
_____
_____
_____
_____
_____
_____
_____
_____

Identify
Describe a risk related to your goals that you did not take.

_____
_____
_____
_____
_____
_____
_____
_____
_____
_____

Why didn't you take the risk (be specific)? Was it fear of failure, fear of embarrassment, fear of success, or something else?

_____
_____
_____
_____
_____
_____
_____

If you had taken the risk and it was successful, how would your life be different?

_____
_____
_____
_____
_____
_____
_____

If you had taken the risk and it failed, what is the worst thing that could have happened? What was the likelihood of that happening?

_____

How could you have recovered from it?

___

Clarify
What have you lost out on or delayed because you were not willing to take a risk?

Why do you believe that you -your dreams, goals and desires, are not worth taking a risk?

How valuable are your dreams, goals and desires to you if you are not willing to take risks to make them a reality?

Are you willing to risk living the rest of your life unfulfilled, dissatisfied, and full of regret?

Yes ___   No ___

Act

If your answer to the last question was no, then make a decision to take a small risk now. Put yourself first for once. Try taking a day off from work to put time and effort into your dreams. I promise you, the company will not fall apart in your absence.

How are you going to put yourself first?

_____
_____
_____
_____
_____
_____
_____
_____

Reach out to someone who could mentor or coach you, or in some way provide some expertise that would help you progress. Who is this person and how can they help you?

_____
_____

Market your product or services. Put it out there, if only to get feedback to help improve what you are doing. So, what are you going to put out there?

Face the fear and do something. What will it be?

It seems to be a law of nature, inflexible and inexorable, that those who will not risk cannot win.

- John Paul Jones

STEP 8

Gaze Over

This seems to be the law of progress in everything we do; it moves along a spiral rather than a perpendicular; we seem to be actually going out of the way, and yet it turns out that we were really moving upward all the time.
- Frances E. Willard

At this point in the game, after Getting Over, Getting On, Getting Obsessed, Giving Out, Grabbing Opportunities, Going On and Gambling Occasionally, you have probably been able to make quite a bit of progress towards your goals. This is the time to stop and Gaze Over where you have come from and how far you have come. Look at how your attitude has changed, how much more confident you are, how strong you are, how much closer you are to your goals. Look at the people who showed up in your life to help you after you made the decision to change your life. Look at the doors that have opened for you since you decided to *GO* for it.

Every now and then, along the path towards your goals, take time to Gaze Over all that is now behind you and that which lies ahead of you. Take a survey of your life and note that when you decided to live the life that you desired and deserved, life rose to meet you where you were and the path before you opened up with each step you took forward in spite of what you saw in front of you. This will help to reenergize you and strengthen you for what lies ahead.

React

What is your immediate reaction to what you've just read? What thoughts came to mind? What feelings did you experience?

_____
_____
_____
_____
_____
_____
_____
_____

Identify

What are some of the decisions you have made recently that are moving you closer to accomplishing your goals?

_____
_____
_____
_____
_____
_____
_____
_____
_____

What are some of the actions you have taken that have helped accelerate your progress?

_____
_____
_____
_____
_____
_____
_____
_____
_____
_____

Who are some of the people you have connected with that have motivated or encouraged you?

_____
_____
_____
_____
_____
_____
_____
_____
_____
_____

List three things that you have accomplished.

_____
_____
_____
_____

___

Clarify

Think about the challenges that you have faced. How does it make you feel to have accomplished what you have in spite of those challenges?

___

Now, think about how much closer you are to your goals. Describe how it feels to know that soon you will be living your dreams.

___

Write below why you deserve this…because you do.

_____
_____
_____
_____
_____
_____
_____
_____
_____

If you don't feel like you have accomplished much, take the time to reassess. Consider how important this goal is to you. Think about how you have been spending your time. Have you really been putting forth the time, energy and effort necessary to accomplish your goals? Have you been caught up with distractions rather than opportunities? How can you get back on track?

_____
_____
_____
_____
_____
_____
_____

Act

Take a deep breath. Now, begin to visualize what it will be like to accomplish your goals. What are you doing? How do you feel? How has it changed your life?

_____
_____
_____
_____
_____
_____
_____
_____
_____
_____
_____
_____
_____
_____
_____
_____
_____
_____
_____
_____
_____
_____
_____
_____

DR. CHERITA WEATHERSPOON

Progress lies not in enhancing what is, but in advancing toward what will be.

- Khalil Gibran

STEP 9

Goof Off

Do what you need to do and enjoy life as it happens.
- John Scalzi

Deciding to *GO* for your goals typically means hard work, persistence and a loss of social and free time. So, every now and then you have to take time to Goof Off.

You do not have to wait until you have accomplished the goal. You need to reward yourself along the way and celebrate small accomplishments that are getting you closer to the overall goal. And, after all, life is about living not just about accomplishing goals. Life should be fun. So make sure that you build some time to Goof Off in your plans. Otherwise, you risk Getting Overwhelmed (not one of the steps in the process, you should avoid this one), having your health impacted by stress, feeling distanced from those closest to you, and maybe even feeling disappointed after you have reached your goal. Have fun, de-stress, take a break.

React
What is your immediate reaction to what you've just read? What thoughts came to mind? What feelings did you experience?

_____
_____
_____
_____
_____
_____
_____
_____
_____

Identify
What do you like to do that you have not been able to do in a while?

_____
_____
_____
_____
_____
_____
_____
_____
_____

Who do you like to spend time with that you have not seen in a long time?

_____
_____
_____
_____
_____
_____
_____
_____
_____

How do you like to treat or pamper yourself?

_____
_____
_____
_____
_____
_____
_____
_____
_____

Clarify
Have you been working hard? How?

_____
_____
_____

GO!

_____
_____
_____
_____
_____
_____

Have you made progress? How?

_____
_____
_____
_____
_____
_____
_____

Have you been consistent? How?

_____
_____
_____
_____
_____
_____
_____
_____

What is keeping you from letting loose and taking time to refresh?

Act

Take some time for yourself. Sleep in late, watch movies all day, go shopping, go out with friends –whatever it is, do something that is fun. Then do something that is relaxing. What are you going to do and when are you going to do it? How often will you do it?

Do something to reward yourself for the progress you have made. What are you going to do and when are you going to do it?

DR. CHERITA WEATHERSPOON

You aren't your work, your accomplishments, your possessions, your home, your family... your anything. You're a creation of your Source, dressed in a physical human body intended to experience and enjoy life on Earth.

- Wayne Dyer

BONUS GIFT

Sometimes we need to hear a little encouragement. Sign up for your complimentary *GO! Motivational Audio* at https://cheritaweatherspoon.com/motivational-audio

STEP 10

Game On

Now the game. Your game. The one that only you [are] meant to play. The one that was given to you when you came into this world. You ready? Take your stance. Don't hold nothing back. Give it everything.
- The Legend of Bagger Vance

Step 10 brings us to a point of new beginnings. Game On. You've accomplished a goal, now I want you to determine the next goal that you are going to commit to working towards today. It does not matter how big or how small it may seem or how important or valuable someone else may think it is. It simply has to be something that YOU want to accomplish and you either have been too afraid to try, you have lacked confidence, other people have talked you out of it or said that you could not do it, or you just have not made time to focus on it. Identify what that next goal is and declare today: Game On.

You've proven that you can play, so be in it to win it. Continue to suit up and get on the field. You cannot win if you do not continue to play. If you play and do not win, you will learn some things that will make you better and stronger for the next game (goal). But you have got to be in the game to have a chance to win the game.

React
What is your immediate reaction to what you've just read? What thoughts came to mind? What feelings did you experience?

_____
_____
_____
_____
_____
_____
_____
_____

Identify
How have you been preparing for this time in your life?

_____
_____
_____
_____
_____
_____
_____
_____
_____

In what ways have you practiced for your turn at success?

_____
_____
_____
_____
_____
_____
_____
_____

Who are your cheerleaders (supporters, motivators, encouragers)?

_____
_____
_____
_____
_____
_____
_____
_____

Who are your coaches (advisors and mentors)?

_____
_____
_____
_____

Who are your fans (people who believe and find value in what you have to offer)?

Clarify
Why is it your time?

Why do you deserve to be successful?

_____
_____
_____
_____
_____
_____
_____
_____
_____

What impact will achieving your goal have on the world?

_____
_____
_____
_____
_____
_____
_____
_____
_____

Act

Get your game face on. Get focused, get serious, get in the game. Minimize your involvement in activities that do not, in some way, contribute to the knowledge and skills you need to accomplish your goals. What are you going to let go of or turn down to focus on what you need to do?

_____
_____
_____
_____
_____
_____
_____

Show up for the game. If you are nervous, show up anyway. If you are afraid, show up ready to play. If you feel like you are not ready, show up and get ready. If other people play better than you, show up ready to learn all that you can. If you play better than everyone else, show up ready to coach. What does showing up look like for you?

_____
_____
_____
_____
_____
_____
_____
_____

Play the game. Get in there and get it done. In spite of obstacles and challenges –play. If you have to be a one person team –play. If you have to coach yourself and cheer for yourself –play. Playing the game is the only possible way to win the game. Winning is what you want; but losing is better than having forfeited –giving up without even trying. Keep playing, eventually you'll end up a champion. Are you ready to play? Game On!

You win some, you lose some, and some get rained out, but you gotta suit up for them all.

- J. Askenberg

Don't Forget Your
Bonus Gifts!

In case you missed them, sign up for your complimentary gifts. These gifts are my way of saying Thank You for making the decision to *GO* after what you want. Your decision to step into your power is going to change your life and the lives of those who are watching you and are impacted by what you will accomplish.

https://cheritaweatherspoon.com/blog-subscription

https://cheritaweatherspoon.com/infographic

https://cheritaweatherspoon.com/motivational-audio

MORE ABOUT THE AUTHOR

Dr. Weatherspoon has been advising, counseling, mentoring and coaching adults through their higher education, personal and career development experiences for over twenty years. As both a Certified Professional Coach and Certified Job & Career Transition Coach, Cherita helps people to clarify, declare and plan their goals; and provides the support and accountability they need for their personal, career and business success. Cherita believes that God has called her to engage others in igniting their passions and pursuing their purpose, elevating their mindsets and perceptions of self, and ultimately empowering them to live a life that reflects their unique power. Thus, Powerhouse Coaching.

Cherita's coaching is transformational. It is not simply about what you want to accomplish. It is about who you want to become. Cherita gets to the heart of the matter - challenging your belief systems, helping you to identify and face your challenges head on, and clarifying your vision of self. She then helps you to identify and navigate the pathways appropriate for you to move forward into your new powerful life. It may result in your seeking new job opportunities or a change in career; perhaps you'll step into entrepreneurship or start a new hobby; maybe you'll begin volunteering or even start a ministry or non-profit organization. Whatever your path may be, Cherita will help you to live a life that aligns with your heart's desire, your God-given talents, your passions, and your purpose. She will help you transform into the powerhouse that you are.

As a consultant, Cherita brings an educational and professional background, which has included leadership in the areas of student support and development, career development, retention, and program development and evaluation that have equipped her with a unique skill set that allows her to flow effortlessly from strategic to tactical perspectives to best serve the organization. Cherita has brought transformation in the areas in which she has served: streamlining processes, reducing expenses, increasing financial resources, improving employee morale, improving client and student outcomes, and leading organizational change effectively. She maintains a successful balance between her tendencies to be goal-oriented and valuing people, being compassionate, fair and just; which makes for an awesome leader.

Cherita finds satisfaction and fulfillment in helping individuals bring their dreams and goals to manifestation and to live the life that they desire and were called to live; and helping organizations to align their mission with their organizational structure, resources and client needs, resulting in greater impact, influence and opportunities for funding.

Cherita is an ordained minister, Educational Specialist, and has earned a bachelor's degree in Business Management, a master's degree in Student Affairs in Higher Education, and a doctorate degree in Educational Leadership. She is also the author of *Community College Leadership Defined: Identifying, Developing and Assessing the Competencies Necessary for Leadership Success in the 21st Century*, a contributing author in *The Gratitude Book Project: Celebrating Moms & Motherhood*, and in the International Best Seller, *My Big Idea Book*.

Cherita is married to a wonderful and supportive husband, and is mother to four beautiful children. She enjoys writing, designing jewelry, and dining out (although she is a very good cook). She is passionate about family, marriage, God, and the detonation of one's personal power.

Connect with Cherita at:
www.CheritaWeatherspoon.com
Facebook: CoachCherita   Instagram: CoachCherita
Twitter: @CoachCherita
YouTube: CheritaWeatherspoon.com/TV

www.ingramcontent.com/pod-product-compliance
Lightning Source LLC
Chambersburg PA
CBHW050541300426
44113CB00012B/2213